D1458309

Dick Walker's

MODERN FLY DRESSINGS

with line drawings by the author,
and colour photographs by Taff Price
from flies tied by Peter Gathercole

Ernest Benn Limited
London & Tonbridge

Other Books by Richard Walker

Still Water Angling
Drop Me a Line
How Fish Feed
Rod Building for Amateurs
Carp Fishing
Walker's Pitch
No Need to Lie
Fly Dressing Innovations
Dick Walker's Angling

Other Books in the
Benn Fishing Handbooks Series

The Super Flies of Still Water
John Goddard

Fifty Favourite Nymphs
T. Donald Overfield

Fifty Favourite Dry Flies
T. Donald Overfield

Floatmaker's Manual
Bill Watson

A Manual of Sea Fishing Baits
Hugh Stoker

British Library Cataloguing in Publication Data

Walker, Dick
  Dick Walker's modern fly dressings.—(Benn
  fishing handbooks).
  1. Fly tying
  2. Trout fishing
  I. Modern fly dressings
  688.7′9   SH451

ISBN 0-510-22536-5

First published 1980 by
Ernest Benn Limited
25 New Street Square, London EC4A 3JA
& Sovereign Way, Tonbridge, Kent TN9 1RW

Filmset by Reproduction Drawing Ltd.,
Sutton, Surrey
Printed in Great Britain
W & J Mackay Limited, Chatham

Introduction

This book is really a continuation of *Fly Dressing Innovations*, which is a collection of the contributions I made to *Trout & Salmon* under the general heading "Modern Trout Fly Dressings." This series has continued and now we have sufficient for another book.

Since *Fly Dressing Innovations* was first published, I have felt able to clarify my theories about why a trout takes an artificial fly, which despite all our efforts is not really very much like the insect it is supposed to imitate.

Trout can be in any of three basic states, between which there may be varying degrees of overlap. The states are these; not feeding; willing to feed but not committed to eating one kind of food exclusively; and selective feeding where only one species of insect or other food form is eaten. Even a fish in the last state may now and then take a different food form, and there is reason to suppose it is more likely to take something very different than something rather less different.

A fish that is not feeding may sometimes be induced to take an artificial or lure through aggression, defence of territory, or of a spawning area.

A fish feeding, but not selectively, is likely if not alarmed, to take almost any sort of artificial fly. A trout feeding selectively is most likely to take an artificial fly in which enough points of resemblance to the real insect have been incorporated. If there are enough of these points, the trout will ignore numerous and blatant points of difference. When one considers how obvious are the differences between a real insect and the best attempt we can make at imitating it, it becomes obvious that this is so. No real insect has a hook-bend, point and barb, nor a hundred legs.

The fly dresser's aim, when tying imitative flies, must be to decide which are the features by which the fish recognises the natural insect, and to incorporate these features where possible. There is good reason to think that some degree of exaggeration of these points can increase the attractiveness of the artificial fly.

I am in no doubt that among the most important features in imitative patterns are colours, and it seems likely that many insects possess what might be called key colours, which are not always obvious, being mixed with other colours in the insect, but still discernible by the fish. Thus, orange in the Blue-winged olive, crimson in the Iron blue, yellow in the Pale watery, green in the Grannom, black and red in the dipteran *Bibio pomonae*, called by some the Bloody butcher, are colours which should be incorporated in imitations of these insects, and if they are exaggerated in area and brightness of colour, the artificials will usually be found more effective for it.

In recent years, a considerable range of synthetic materials has been made available to fly dressers. Tying threads of nylon and terylene (dacron) are superior to silk, but whether some of the other materials can help to produce more killing fies than natural feathers, furs and wools is less certain. Time will tell.

From time to time, ideas like detached bodies, hooks for flies tied to fish hook-pint up, hooks intended to avoid catching snags, dry flies tied with wings and hackles at the bend instead of just behind the eye, and other ingenious notions, are re-invented. None of them has been proved advantageous, most of them were tried and discarded in the last century, and some have definite disadvantages. If you want a fly to drag across the bottom of the lake or river, bind some layers of lead foil to the back of the shank and dress the fly over them.

May I conclude by thanking all the friends, including readers and Editorial staff of *Trout & Salmon*, who have helped me to compile this list of fly patterns?

Richard Walker

Contents

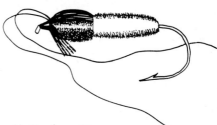

1 The Small Sedge Pupa

This is a pattern that is often successful when the smaller kinds of sedge-fly are hatching, both on rivers and lakes. For river work, it is fished as one would a fast-sinking nymph; on stillwaters, a sink-and-draw action is used.

Two layers of lead foil from a wine-bottle top are lashed to the top of the hook-shank and then covered with the dressing which is as follows:

Hook	No 12 or 14
Abdomen	Dyed feather-fibre wound over the varnished tying silk while the varnish is wet
Thorax	Sepia feather-fibre
Hackle and wing cases	Fibres from a speckled grouse feather
Antennae	Dark brown horse-hair

The most effective colours for the abdomen are grass-green, pale blue-green, and amber.

The trick for fixing the wing-cases and hackle is to tie in the grouse fibres at the junction of abdomen and thorax, before the thorax is wound, with their tips projecting sufficiently far ahead of the hook eye to be drawn back and secured, before the rest of the fibres are pulled forward and tied down over the thorax.

The horsehair is tied round the shank just behind the eye with a single overhand knot and disposed, while finishing the head, so as to project forwards, though it trails backwards in the water to imitate the two long antennae of the natural. Each antenna should be about twice the length of the hook.

2 The Bumblebee

In every trout-fisher's fly-box, there should be at least one crazy, unorthodox pattern, which he would not, in the ordinary course of events, even dream of using. This pattern, if ever used, would be tried in desperation after everything else had failed. It is sometimes remarkable how, in such circumstances, the ridiculous fly will catch fish after fish. Remember H. T. Sheringham with the Bottle Brush, and A. Courtney Williams with the artificial spider?

So here is a dressing for you to try when the trout have refused everything else you can think of.

Hook	Size 6 round bend
Abdomen	Rings of white, black and amber ostrich herl, tied very fat and clipped short, over special underbody
Thorax	Black ostrich herl, clipped short
Wings	Plymouth Rock (cuckoo) hackle points, tied flat, sloping backwards
Legs	Pheasant tail fibres dyed black, knotted and cut short
Hackle	None

To bulk out body and thorax, bind a little bit of matchstick, tapered at both ends, to the back of the hook-shank. That, whipped over with floss and then with the dyed ostrich herl, makes a fat body without filling up the gape of the hook too much.

The order of colours for the abdomen, reading from the rear end, is white, black, amber, black.

The fly is fished dry. It is deadly for chub and will sometimes bring a trout up in clear water, when smaller flies, either sunk or floating, have failed. It also impresses non-anglers greatly!

8

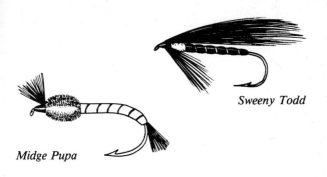

Sweeny Todd

Midge Pupa

3 Five Flies for Still Waters

Several readers who have recently taken up fly-tying have asked me to select a series of patterns for stillwater trout fishing which they can tie during the winter when they can't fish. So now, instead of describing another pattern, I am giving a list of the most useful flies, in the certain knowledge that those who tie them will find themselves fishing among anglers who are catching fish after fish on a pattern that I have failed to include. I shall then be blamed for the omission!

Stillwater flies fall into various categories. First comes insect imitation, of which the most important are midge pupae. Tie these: Black in sizes 16, 12 and 10; Claret in size 12; Green in sizes 16 and 12; Orange, size 12; Olive size 10; Gold-ribbed Olive, size 12. I tend to think that a Black Pupa imitation with the rear two segments crimson will replace both Black and Claret Pupae, but this remains unproven.

Next, Sedge Pupae: tie yourself some Green and some Amber Longhorns, size 10, or, if you prefer to be more conventional, some Invictas of the same size, with or without red tails.

On stillwaters where ephemerid flies are found, a few Olive Nymphs, size 14, will be useful.

There are many other insect imitations that I could list, but none so important as the above.

The second category is dry flies: tie Daddy-long-legs on a size 10 longshank, Red Sedge on a size 10 normal shank, and Dronefly on a size 12. Again, there are others, but none so useful as these three.

The third category is that of lures. I have abandoned multi-hook lures and I much prefer hair wings to those made of cock hackles. My choice in hairwings is Sweeny Todd, Whisky fly, and Mrs. Palmer. The last is a comparatively recent innovation, but one that has proved a deadly killer, because it can stand being fished more slowly than any other lure I know, and still attract trout. Don't let the professionals fob you off with bright yellow hair, or coarse bucktail, for the wing. The correct colour is very pale yellow and the hair must be fine and silky goat hair. These lures are all dressed on size 8 and size 6 longshanks. I like the hairwing to extend well beyond the hook-bend.

In the fourth category there are fry-flies. I'd suggest a brown-backed Polystickle for normal conditions; an orange-backed one for mud-stains, and a white PVC-bodied one for late evening. They can all be dressed on size 6 long-shanks, silvered for choice.

The fifth category consists of heavily-leaded flies, mainly for use on smaller stillwaters where you can see the trout. Tie Leaded Shrimps in dark brown-olive, pale olive and bright orange. You can then choose whichever shows best against the bottom. Tie these on size 10 hooks, and some heavily leaded Corixae with pale yellow bodies and green-olive backs.

The above dressings, to be found in any recognised book on the subject, constitute the backbone of my stillwater selection wherever I fish. Of course there are many, many more, but a stillwater angler with these will seldom find himself unable to catch fish for lack of a suitable pattern.

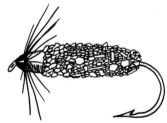

4 The Artificial Caddis

Artificial caddises are quite easy to make and can often be very effective, especially when trout are feeding near the bottom of heavy, fast water. You simply cast and allow the caddis to trundle along the bottom. When a trout takes it, there is usually ample time to tighten, since the artificial feels like the real caddis, which the fish is in the habit of swallowing whole.

To make the caddis, build up a fat body of floss, cream or white in colour, on a size 10 long-shank hook. Soak this body in Vycoat, and while it is still wet, shake it in a tin full of clean, dry, fine sand. Leave it overnight to set, then put on a few turns of amber or light green wool at the head end, followed by a couple of turns of any soft, short-fibred black hackle. Complete the fly with a fat black head, well varnished.

To prepare suitable sand, collect a sample—roadside gutters after rain offer a good source of supply—wash it well under the tap (which will remove soluble material and any soft, light stuff), and then spread it out, dry it thoroughly, and put it through a fine-mesh cooks' sieve to remove the larger pieces. Tiny stones stick very firmly to the Vycoat, and you may have to pick off a few of the little stones before putting on the wool, hackle and head.

Do not fish this pattern on leader points finer than about 6 lb bs (1x), for it is heavy and quickly fatigues anything finer.

5 The Mayfly

The first mention I can find of the efficacy of hot orange in Mayfly dressings is in Major Courtney Williams' *Dictionary of Trout Flies,* in which a pattern known as Goulden's Favourite is described. There can be no doubt that in certain circumstances, the presence of the orange hackle in a Mayfly pattern makes it especially attractive to trout.

My experience is that this kind of Mayfly is not as good as some other patterns when a normal hatch of naturals is in progress and the trout are eating most of the naturals that come over them or are to be found in their path; but when the hatch is very heavy and the trout are able to eat only a small percentage of the insects, then the artificial with the orange hackle will kill, fish often passing by several naturals to reach it.

The orange-hackled Mayfly is also useful for trout that have become suspicious of other patterns, through being hooked and lost, or pricked.

An orange-dyed cock hackle can be added to any good pattern that imitates the sub-imago, but I generally tie a hackle fly as follows, the variations depending on materials available.

Hook	Size 8 or 10 round-bend long-shank
Tails	Pheasant-tail fibres
Body	Very pale buff turkey-tail fibres or suitable substitute, with two bands of pheasant tail at rear end, as illustrated
Hackles	One short-fibred hot-orange cock hackle wound directly behind the eye. Behind that, either one green-dyed cock hackle and one French partridge hackle, or one speckled duck feather, wound as a hackle, plus one green-dyed cock hackle; or one speckled duck feather, dyed greendrake colour, wound as a hackle, plus one ginger cock hackle.

All three versions are equally effective.

6 The Point-Up Leaded Nymph

This dressing is intended to minimise two of the difficulties encountered in nymph-fishing.

One is that when fishing upstream in deep, fast water, either the nymph fails to sink sufficiently deeply by the time it comes to the fish, or else it has to be cast a long way upstream of the fish, with decreased accuracy and risk of the heavy fly-line coming into the fish's view.

The other is that if heavily-leaded nymphs are used to obviate the first difficulty, they tend to catch up in weed or on the bottom.

The remedy is to use lead to bias the nymph to fish hook-point up, and this is done by binding narrow strips of lead foil on the back of the hook-shank. I find that with size 16 and 14 hooks, one long strip from just behind the eye to the beginning of the bend can be bound on, and three more short strips can then be attached, one above the other, where the thorax and wing cases will be.

The nymph is then dressed as usual, though an increase in the amount and the length of the throat hackle still further encourages the nymph to fish point-up.

Pheasant-tail fibre is far more durable than any other for the bodies and tails of nymphs for river fishing, so much so that if you want colours other than natural pheasant tail, it pays to bleach and dye pheasant tail rather than use other kinds of feather fibre.

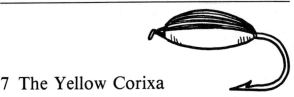

7 The Yellow Corixa

During 1973 I fished a number of man-made trout fisheries of the sort that, happily, are being made in increasing numbers. Among them were Damerham, and Latimer Lakes, in both of which I found quite large numbers of a small corixa that had bright yellow under-parts and an olive-green back. Autopsies showed the trout to be very fond of these animals, so I tied some simple imitations that proved very successful.

The dressing could hardly be simpler: Primrose floss for the body; olive-green feather-fibre for the back. Since there is no wing or hackle to get clogged up, I improved the durability of the fly by soaking it in clear varnish.

I put two strips of lead foil, one above the other, on the back of the hookshank underneath the floss. This takes the Corixa down quickly and makes it fish point-up, so it doesn't catch the bottom. I fished it on a floating line, let it sink right to the bottom, and pulled it up when I saw a trout cruising by.

The hook is No 14 and the silk yellow.

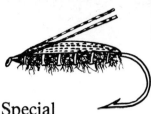

8 The Mead Mill Special

This is a pattern I devised mainly for catching grayling, for which it proved very successful. The first time I tried it was at Mead Mill on the Test, hence its name, but it has also done well for grayling on the upper Avon.

With half-a-dozen of these patterns in my box, the time came when I tried them on trout, and found they were equally successful. I imagine fish take them either for caddis in their cases or perhaps for free-swimming sedge pupae. Whatever they are taken for, taken they very often are, and the lead ensures they get well down to fish feeding on or near the bottom.

The dressing is as follows:

Hook	No. 12 or No. 10, normal shank
Silk	Olive
Body	Three parts grass green wool thoroughly mixed with one part lime green DRF wool, dubbed on the silk and ribbed with fine gold thread
Back	Fibres from a speckled turkey tail feather, tied in at head and tail
Legs	Two fibres of the back material, as illustrated

Before the dressing is commenced, three strips of wine bottle lead foil are bound one above the other on the back of the hook-shank, each successive piece being fractionally shorter and wider than its predecessor. This not only makes the fly sink quickly, but also to fish hook-point upwards so that it seldom catches in the bottom or on weed.

9 The Leadhead

The Leadhead is a pattern that may be dressed in a variety of colour combinations. Its advantages are that it can be fished deep on a floating fly-line, retrieved at a modest pace, and that it seldom catches weed or snags, as it fishes hook-point upwards.

It is dressed as follows: On a No 8 or No 10 forged round-bend hook, pinch a split shot, BB or a little smaller just behind the eye. Use pliers to pinch the shot on firmly.

Between the eye and the shot, and also behind the eye, build up tapered bindings of tight turns, and soak these bindings with PVC varnish (Vycoat), make a body of floss, ribbed with tinsel, on the hook-shank, and tie in a bunch of suitable hair to form a wing. Varnish over the head and the bindings, including that which holds the wing, until all is smooth and glossy. Then paint the head with plastic paint and, when this is dry, apply a spot of white plastic paint on each side, followed by one of black, smaller, to make a pair of eyes.

Finally, give the entire head an extra coat of clear PVC varnish.

Useful colours are: Yellow wing, light brown head, arc chrome DF wool or floss body; black head, wing, and body, ribbed silver thread; natural grey squirrel wing, brown head, red DF wool body; grey squirrel dyed yellow wing, brown head, red DF wool body.

I have no doubt that there are many other combinations of colours that would prove effective.

The Leadhead is fished by casting it out, on a leader of appropriate length, allowing it to sink to the desired depth, and retrieving it in either short jerks or long pulls with pauses in between.

It is essential that a hook with a forged or flattened shank be used, otherwise the shot will rotate round the shank, and the centre of the shot must be well above the shank. This, combined with a downturned eye, ensures that the Leadhead fishes point-up. With shot smaller than BB, it is better to tie the wing on the inside of the hook-shank.

10 The Red-and-Black Midge Pupa

Among the more common species of midge or buzzer is the
family of black ones, which range in size from some too
small to imitate to quite large ones whose imitations can be
tied on hooks as large as No 10. Most, if not all, of these
black buzzers start life as bright red bloodworms, some of
whose crimson coloration is retained when the larva
changes to a pupa, though this is not usually apparent
unless the natural is held up to the light.

Because of this, I began tying artificial black midge
pupae with the rearmost two segments red, and these
caught trout very well. More recently, I have tried some
that were sent to me by the Rev. R. J. Redrup, in which the
abdomens consisted of crimson and natural black feather-
fibre, twisted together before being wound round the hook-
shank. These were every bit as successful as my red-ended
pattern and are easier to tie. The dressing is:

Hook	10 to 16
Abdomen	One strand of crimson-dyed swan feather-fibre, plus two strands natural black feather-fibre, twisted together
Rib	White cock hackle stalk
Thorax	Natural black feather-fibre, or bronze peacock herl, wound fat
Breathing tubes (head and tail)	Bunches of white cock hackle fibres, clipped to length

Start the abdomen about one-third of the way round the
bend.

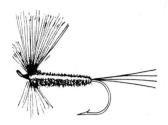

11 The Woolly B-W.O.

A letter from Mr F. G. Baker in the May 1974 issue of *Trout and Salmon* prompts me to describe a new dressing for the blue-winged olive *(Ephemerella ignita)* which I have found considerably more successful than any other.

It can be tied either as a hackled or a winged pattern. In the first case the hackle and whisks are dark slate-coloured cock; in the second these are brownish-olive, with wings of coot feather fibre, or of cock hackle fibres dyed dark slate-colour.

What is important is the body, which is made of equal parts of hot orange and bright blue fine lamb's wool, thoroughly mixed and dubbed on hot-orange tying silk. Knitting wool won't do, even if teased out. You want natural wool clipped or shaved from a sheep's belly. When the two wools are mixed, the dubbing appears to be a yellowish-green, like the body of the natural insect. Meticulous fly-tyers will mix the wools, and choose their individual shades, so as to match the insect's colour; but the use of mixed blue and orange wools is important; the substitution of wool dyed yellowish-green throughout does not seem to be satisfactory.

A female b-w.o. sub-imago has a bright orange body encased in a translucent blue skin, giving the characteristic yellowish-green appearance. It seems possible that the trout is able to see these colours separately. However that may be, the body I have described is usually acceptable to fish eating newly-hatched b-w.o.s.

Until the advent of modern waterproofing agents, wool bodies were not very satisfactory for dry flies, but now we can use them freely, we may find other cases where bodies of mixed colours prove more effective than those of a single colour.

12 The Leaded D.F. Doll

Two or three seasons ago, Bob Church introduced a fly which he called the Baby Doll. It consisted of a fat body made of daylight-fluorescent white wool, with the same material tied in to form a back and tail.

The Baby Doll has proved very successful; but I could never quite see the purpose of the back, which is the same colour as the body. I therefore experimented with a simpler dressing, in which the back was omitted. This seemed every bit as attractive to trout. Later, I introduced some lead to increase the sinking rate and to cause the thing to fish hook-point up, which goes a long way towards preventing the hook catching bottom, or snags, when fished deep. This version has been remarkably successful.

This is how it is made.

Just behind the eye of a No 6 or No 8 longshank hook, tie in a length of daylight-fluorescent white wool with white tying silk, having varnished the hook-shank with 'Vycoat' to prevent iron stain.

Let the short end of the wool lie along the shank, projecting beyond the bend. Over this, wind the longer end of the wool in close, tight turns. Having reached the beginning of the bend, wind the wool back over itself. Continue winding back and forth, keeping the turns very close towards the middle of the fish-shaped body you are building up, but not so close at the ends; this will give a nice cigar-shape.

When you see that the point has been reached where only one more layer of wool is required, take three strips of wine-bottle lead foil, each a little wider than the thickness of the body, and lay them lengthwise along the top of the body, binding them down firmly with the final layer of white wool, which should finish just behind the eye, where the white tying silk secures it.

Then tie in above the body a false hackle of either crimson or orange dyed cock hackle, and finish the head. This hackle should be very short. Varnish the head, and clip the tail to length.

Then take a piece of fine glass-paper and rub the body all over, to fluff up the wool and make it look velvety. This is important, and gives most of the fluorescent effect.

This fly can be fished very slowly, or even allowed to lie inert on the bottom, from which trout frequently pick it up.

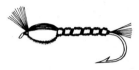

13 The Jumbo Pupa

When one is fishing from a boat in comparatively calm conditions on large, rich reservoirs, it is not uncommon to find a few large dark insects hovering close by. They have their abdomens curved in the form characteristic of chironomids, but they are far larger than any of the midges one sees on the water. They are also extremely agile, and I have never been able to catch one, nor have I found one inside a trout.

What I have found in trout is a very large and striking creature which I suspect is the pupa of the airborne animal described above. Some of these pupae were still alive, and I do not think their colours had been affected. They had dark olive-brown thoraces, medium olive abdomens with crimson segmentation, and the usual whitish appendages at head and tail.

An imitation which I tied has been successful. I call it the Jumbo Pupa, and the dressing is as follows:

Hook   No 8 long-shank
Abdomen   Green-olive feather-fibre ribbed with crimson floss
Thorax and wing-cases Dark brown-olive feather-fibre
Tail and head appendages White cock hackle fibres, clipped to length

The crimson floss should be soaked in dilute cellulose varnish before tying in, to prevent its dye spreading to the feather-fibre when the fly has been wetted.

19

The 'Woolly' Mayfly Nymph from above

14 A New Mayfly Nymph

Early in my series in *Trout and Salmon* I gave a dressing for the Mayfly nymph that caught a lot of fish, but was somewhat complicated and time-consuming to tie. Later I was able to describe a second pattern that caught trout equally well but was very much simpler to tie.

Both these patterns used ostrich herl as the main material, however, and there is no denying that this is rather easily cut by trout teeth. Last winter, therefore, I sought for means of producing a more durable Mayfly nymph. This is perhaps the most successful leaded nymph ever devised for the smaller stillwaters, having in the last few years caught literally thousands of trout, including a good many in the teens of pounds, and up to 20 lb, even on waters where no real mayflies exist. It also kills well on most rivers.

The main difference between it and the earlier patterns is that wool replaces the ostrich herl, and that the body and thorax are strengthened by means of PVC varnish (Vycoat). The procedure is:

Build up an underbody on a No 8 long-shank, down-eyed hook, either with floss or, if a leaded nymph is required, with successive strips of lead foil on the top of the shank, running lengthwise. In actual fishing the leaded version is almost always the one you need to use, and placing the lead foil on the top, or back, of the shank causes the nymph to fish hook-point upwards. The number of strips you use depends on the thickness of your lead foil, but four or five strips of the sort found on good quality wine-bottles is about right. Each strip is bound on with tying silk; neat, close turns are not necessary.

Having built up the under-body, running from just ahead of the beginning of the bend to just behind the eye, tie in at the tail four or five strands of pheasant tail fibre to make the short tails; one strand of medium warm brown nylon thread, and a strand of very pale buff knitting wool. Carry the tying silk back to a point about three-fifths of the way to the eye.

Wind the wool in close turns to this point and secure with the silk, but do not cut off the end of the wool. Then wind on the nylon thread as a ribbing, in a special way, which consists in making about five close turns of the nylon near the rear end of the body (or abdomen) followed by a small space, then four close turns, then a series of open spirals until you reach the point at which the wool has been tied down. There tie off the ribbing—which should have been wound on the opposite spiral to the wool.

The two sets of close turns of ribbing near the rear of the abdomen imitate the dark bands on the natural insect.

Next, tie in a bunch of pheasant tail fibres with their points extending far enough beyond the eye to bend back in two bunches to form legs; but before doing that, wind on the wool to form the thorax, tie down and cut off the waste. Then divide the pheasant tail fibres into two backward-sloping horizontal bunches. Finally, bring the butts of the pheasant tail fibres forwards, tie down to form wing-cases, and finish the head.

Now prick out the wool between each open turn of the ribbing on each side of the abdomen, with a dubbing needle. Pull out quite a considerable piece of wool fibre at each point. Then clip these bunches of projecting wool with scissors so that all are of equal length.

Finally, run a streak of clear PVC varnish along the upper and lower sides of the abdomen and the underside of the thorax. This sticks the wool down solidly, but leaves the projecting tufts of wool unvarnished and free to move in the water. The result is a tremendously durable nymph; I have one that has taken 17 trout and is still intact.

While the winged Mayfly is in evidence for only about three weeks, the nymphs are present in the river or lake from a few weeks after the hatch (when they are very tiny) until the hatch of the following year. Consequently, while the main use of the artificial nymph, in size 8, is from the beginning of May until the middle of June, much smaller examples of the same pattern will catch trout and grayling from about the beginning of August onwards.

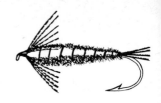

15 The Lamb's-Wool Damsel Nymph

There can be very few stillwater trout fisheries where damsel flies are not found, and although they are never sufficiently numerous to form an important element in the diet of the trout, it is not uncommon to find them in trout stomachs.

An imitation of the damsel nymph will sometimes catch a fish or two, and the success of Mr Alan Pearson's Green Beast may be due to its resemblance to a damsel nymph. However, some months ago, while tying Blue-winged Olives with bodies of well-mixed orange and blue lamb's-wool, it occurred to me to tie one or two damsel nymphs with the same dubbing.

My first opportunity to try the pattern occurred at Damerham in early August. I caught 23 trout in two afternoons and one whole day. Eight of the fish were over 4 lb and one 5 lb; and all but one were taken on the Lamb's-Wool Damsel Nymph.

The dressing is as follows:

Hook	No 8 long shank, loaded with three longitudinal strips of lead foil
Tails	Four or five strands of pale pheasant tail fibres, dyed green, short
Body	A mixture of equal parts of bright orange and cobalt blue lamb's-wool, dubbed on pale brown silk. Increase the thickness of the dubbing as you wind from tail to head, so as to produce a carrot-shaped body
Rib	Pale brown 'silk' in Terylene
Hackle	Sparse grey partridge (speckled) dyed grass-green

I caught my fish by allowing the nymph to sink right to the bottom, then tweaking it back fairly slowly.

16 Mother's Doormat

This pattern was invented by Mr Bob Underwood, who has had considerable success with it in the smaller stillwater trout fisheries, especially at Fairoak in Hampshire. It evidently imitates a sedge pupa, and has much in common with the Amber Nymph. However, a score of 173 trout caught with it in the 1974 season by Mr Underwood is enough to commend it as a valuable pattern in its own right.

It received its name from the material used for the abdomen, although it came from a piece of woollen carpet rather than the usual hairy doormat. The colour is amber (officially described as 'Californian Orange'), and it is dubbed on the yellow tying silk. A piece of white polythene strip is tied in at the tail, then brought forward and tied in at the junction of abdomen and thorax.

The thorax, in the samples given me, is of dark red cotton, wound very bulkily, but I think it would be equally effective to make it of dubbed dark red wool, thus saving tying time.

The hook size is 12 or 10, normal shank. Some lead can be incorporated under the dressing, if desired.

---

17 Flies Without Feathers

Some time ago the Editor of *Trout and Salmon* received a letter from a reader whose friend is allergic to feathers to the extent that it is out of the question for him to use any artificial fly into whose construction feathers are incorporated. The reader wished to know what could be done about it, so the Editor asked me. I not only had a shot at solving the problem myself, but also dragged Miss Jacqueline Wakeford and Mr David Collyer into it.

I think the first reaction of all three of us was to consult the late W. H. Lawrie's book *All-fur flies and how to dress them*. I am sorry to report that it was of no use; the method therein described, of how to make a dry-fly hackle with fur fibres, just isn't practical.

Miss Wakeford made some very pretty Olives and Iron Blues with clipped deer-hair hackles—on the lines of a Muddler Minnow head but much more sparse. These flies floated beautifully.

David Collyer managed to produce some nice flies with fine hair fibres, such as squirrel. How he got them to spread radially, I don't know, but he did it, though he tells me it was a rather tedious business.

I messed about, making some bad hair dry flies that I would have been ashamed for anyone to see, until I hit on an idea that works remarkably well and is easy and quick to execute. It can be used for ephemerid and sedge imitations, and is not confined to hair; feather-fibre, especially cock hackle fibre, can also be used.

I will describe a sedge imitation first because that is easiest. Put the hook in the vice and make the body of the fly exactly as you would for a normal pattern. Then take a bunch of fibres of the appropriate colour; fine hair or cock hackle fibres, it doesn't matter which if you aren't allergic. Tie the bunch on the back of the hook-shank between the forward end of the body and the hook-eye, very firmly, with the thinner ends of the fibres pointing backwards, towards the hook-bend.

Then divide the roots of the fibres into two equal bunches and set them so that they project approximately horizontally, at right angles to the hook-shank, one bunch on each side. You do this by means of a figure-of-eight binding with the tying silk. You will find that the fibres fan out quite a lot, which is very desirable.

If you have judged correctly the length of those fibres that are left pointing backwards over the hook-bend, you can leave them as they are. I prefer to tie them over-long and clip them square, level with the hook-bend.

The two horizontal bunches are also clipped, and you will find that they can be clipped very short and still float the fly well. They are not dissimilar to Parachute hackles in effect, but disposed as they are, they don't have to be very long. The fly is finished by adding a tiny amount of suitable dubbing on the silk and winding this over the figure-of-eight binding, before finishing the head. This gives a little extra bulk to the thorax. It isn't absolutely necessary, but the finished fly looks nicer if those figure-of-eight bindings are concealed by this little bit of dubbing.

You do a whip-finish behind the eye as with any other fly. The fibres will never slip, bent at right angles as they are.

An ephemerid imitation is produced in much the same way, except that the bunch of fibres is tied in before the body is made. Here it is important to leave the sharp ends of the fibres the right length, because the next step is to set them up vertical, or nearly so, with turns of silk behind them. Having done that, make the body and tails as usual, and then divide the roots of the fibres as explained for the sedge pattern, and secure them in two horizontal bunches with a figure-of-eight binding.

Alternatively, you can tie in the fibres with their pointed ends forward, setting them up in the advanced-wing style. Divide the roots to make the two horizontal bunches before proceeding with the body and tails.

As with the sedge pattern, these horizontal bunches can be clipped quite short. Experiments in actual fishing will teach you just how short they can be. Some hairs and hackle-fibres are what might be called 'two-tone', and with these, tied in at the right point relative to their colour division, you can produce flies with wings of one colour and horizontal 'hackles' of another.

With practice, I find I can tie flies in this style in about two-thirds of the time it would take to tie conventional winged dry flies. Quickest of all is a spent spinner. All you do for that is tie in a bunch of fibres of appropriate colour with their points forward; clip off the butts on the slant and form the body, which will cover the butts. Tie in tails as usual.

Then simply divide the forward-projecting fibres into two equal bunches and use a figure-of-eight binding to set them horizontal and at right angles to the hook-shank. A little dubbing on the last turns of the figure-of-eight makes the thorax.

No extra hackle is needed to make such a fly float beautifully, with the fibre wings supporting it in or on the surface film. This idea is not new, however; it was first used for the Henderson Spent Mayfly.

Any suitable material can be used for bodies in all these flies, but for quick production there is a lot to be said for fine wool or fur dubbing, since the same stuff as is used for the body can also be used, very thinly applied, to cover the figure-of-eight bindings that divide the hair or fur fibres that make the wing and hackles.

Fur should be bought on the skin; not only is it much easier to clip out a bunch, but most furs on the skin provide three different sorts of fibre. The longest are the guard hairs and these can be picked out, in many cases, without disturbing the other hairs. Next longest are the main hairs, but below these is the soft under-fur, which is often useful for dubbing, either by itself or blended.

I cannot claim phenomenal catches with flies dressed as described, because the idea came too recently to permit proper trials in actual fishing. All I can say is that they float beautifully, look good on the water whether viewed from above or below the surface, and are very easily tied and exceptionally durable, especially when dressed with hair rather than hackle fibre.

18 The Hairwing Spent Mayfly

Imitations of the spent female Mayfly are numerous, but most of them suffer from the drawbacks associated with wings made from either cock or hen hackle-points. These tend to bend back and catch the bend of the hook; and their stalks not uncommonly break. In addition, unless these wings are positioned very accurately, they may cause the fly to spin in the air and put twists in the leader.

Two patterns avoid this trouble. They are Henderson's Spent Mayfly, the wings of which are bunches of hackle fibres, and Barrett's Shaving Brush, which has wings of badger hair. My experience of the former is that the hackle fibres tend to stick soggily together, while the inherent stiffness of the badger hair in the latter makes the pattern difficult to tie and hard for fish to suck in.

I have, therefore, been experimenting, and I now have a spent pattern that seems to me to offer some advantages. The dressing is as follows:

Hook	No 8 long shank
Tails	Pheasant-tail fibres dyed sepia
Body	Ivory-coloured wool, with two bands of dark brown wool near the rear of the body, as shown in the illustration
Rib	Sepia tying silk
Wings	Black squirrel tail hair, secured in two horizontal bunches with figure-of-eight binding
Thorax	Sepia pheasant-tail fibres
Hackle	None

The first tying operation consists of tying in a bunch of squirrel-tail hairs with their points forwards, over the eye. Fluff these fibres so that they vary in length. Cut the roots slantwise so that what is left varies in length, the longest remaining being short of the start of the bend. Carry the silk over these hair butts to the start of the bend, when you tie in the tails, body materials and rib. Then carry the silk back to the shoulder. Next, wind the body and rib, and tie in the fibres for the thorax.

Carry out the figure-of-eight binding to set the squirrel fibres in two horizontal bunches; then varnish the binding and wind the sepia pheasant fibre over it to form the thorax. Then whip finish.

Choose for the wings a squirrel tail that is not completely black, but has a dappled or speckled effect. Many so-called black squirrel tails are thus.

No hackle is needed; a dip in a silicone-wax floatant will ensure the fly floats well. It is an exceptionally durable pattern and will neither spin in the air nor catch its wings under the hook bend.

The sketch is a plan view.

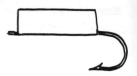

19 The Filtip

This is a dry fly that can sometimes be very effective. It imitates an insect that is often seen on trout waters, especially those I fish. Its scientific name is *Fagendus vulgaris,* and it is in its spent stage that it is most often taken by trout. A similar insect, *Fagendus corktippus,* is also seen at times, but I have not yet produced an imitation of it.

When *Fagendus vulgaris* is on the water, it is not at all uncommon to see a trout come up and take it. When this is noticed, tie a Filtip to your leader point, cast it out and let it lie on the surface. When it is taken, tighten at once, as it is quickly ejected.

The dressing is simple. Take a straight-eyed No 8 long-shank hook and push its eye lengthwise through a filter-tip from a 'Consulate' cigarette; not through the middle, but close to the side. Give the fly several coats of Vycoat, which will waterproof it, when it will float without needing any further water-proofing.

I cannot claim that the Filtip has accounted for the 50 trout that would normally qualify a pattern for inclusion here. Its score is in fact five.

20 Green Rabbits

This is a useful pattern on both still and running waters, and it has the merit of being easily and quickly tied. Useful sizes are from 14 to 10, but a big one on a No 8 long shank is sometimes very effective on stillwaters, especially if it has three or four layers of lead foil bound to the back of the shank, underneath the dressing, which is as follows:

Tails   Five or six strands of any brown or buff feather, rather short

Body	One part teased-out lime green d.f. wool to two parts wild rabbit back fur, thoroughly well mixed and dubbed on light silk. Prick out the dubbing to produce hairy-looking body
Rib	Fine gold thread
Hackle	Brown partridge, short in fibre, or cut short

On stillwaters, cast the Rabbit out, allow it to sink, then retrieve with long, slow pulls. In running water fish it like a nymph. The No 12 and 14 sizes are good for grayling, especially if leaded.

21 Multi-Muddler

The Multi-Muddler is a cross between a Muddler Minnow and a tube fly.

You build a Muddler Minnow head, made in the usual way from deer-hair, on a short length of thin tube. This can be plastic, aluminium or brass, depending on how you want your fly to fish.

The head, dressed on the tube, is threaded on the line, which is then knotted to the eye of any fly you want to use. This will usually be a bucktail, hairwing or streamer lure, and should have a straight eye.

After spinning the deer-hair on the tube, it should be clipped so that the rearmost hairs are a little longer. They then cover the eye and head of the fly.

A selection of these heads tied in different sizes, and on tubes of different kinds, provides the angler with a wide range of possible combinations. Using a head on a brass tube gives a diving lure that can be deadly at times.

The articulation between the head and the fly gives an attractive waggling motion.

22 The Zero

I am indebted to Mr Steve Parton for this hairwing pattern, which is representative of a variety of recently-introduced hairwing lures whose predominant colour is white.

The specimen that Mr Parton sent me is tied on a 1/0 silvered round-bend hook but he tells me that ideally it should be tied on a 4/0 fine-wire, silvered flounder hook.

The dressing is as follows:

Tail	Hot-orange calf tail hair
Body	Heavy white daylight fluorescent chenille
Rib	Wide embossed silver tinsel
Throat hackle	White goat hair, tied 'false'
Wing	Composite; white goat hair with silver ba-boon hair above and three white cock sad-dle hackles on each side. Cock up the wing so that its top makes an angle of about 45 degrees to the body
Head	Black, with eye painted on

Fish this lure deep and move it in steady draws of about a foot at a time. Do not strip fast. The Zero is intended to imitate bream-fry, which are quite numerous at Grafham. Where roach-fry are commoner, as at Chew, it might be a good idea to make both tail and throat hackles crimson.

The sketch is diagrammatic—you can't show a predominantly white fly very well when you have to draw in black on a white background!

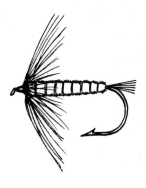

23 The Blue Midge

There are times when trout behave in a manner which can perhaps be described as 'gobbling'. In stillwaters they swim around, opening and closing their mouths quite quickly, their nebs breaking the surface most of the time. This feeding action is less common in rivers, but it does sometimes take place, the difference being that the trout maintains its station.

I am by no means sure which food-form provokes such behaviour, and it is possible that it occurs with more than one kind of insect or other organism; but I do have a pattern of artificial fly that often—though not always—succeeds when trout are 'gobbling'.

Here is the dressing:

Hook	14 and 16
Tails	A bunch of white cock hackle fibres, cut short
Body	Palest heron herl
Rib	White cock hackle stalk
Hackle	Soft dun cock

Do not grease the leader when fishing this pattern. It is very light and if you start a slow retrieve as soon as the fly is in the water—if fishing stillwaters—it will stay within ½ in of the surface. In running water, let it go down the current without drag. If fish refuse the size 14, try the 16.

24 The Ladybird

This is a useful pattern to carry, although opportunities to use it effectively are not frequent. However, there are times when very large numbers of ladybirds get on to the waters of lakes and reservoirs, and I have found trout stomachs packed with them.

In river fishing, trout rising under trees will often accept an artificial ladybird, though an imitation green caterpillar is more often successful in such circumstances.

In addition to ladybirds, there are other beetles of similar size and shape, but with metallic blue-black wing covers, that also find their way onto the water in quantities at times. To imitate these, a similar tie is used, but with a piece of metallic blue feather from a mallard drake wing instead of pheasant tail for the wing covers.

The dressing for the Ladybird is as follows:

Hook	Size 14
Body	Bronze peacock herl tied fat
Hackle	Short, sparse natural black cock. (Clip it short)
Wing covers	Bright chestnut pheasant tail fibres There is no need to imitate the spots

Soak the fly in silicone-wax fly-flotant and fish it dry.

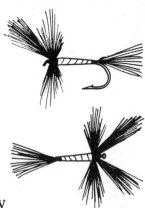

25 Russell's Mayfly

Pat Russell, of Romsey, has developed a new and remarkably effective artificial Mayfly. The idea was sparked off by a pattern given him by Frank Speak, which resembled a large Red Wulff. This was progressively modified to become the pattern that Pat uses with such success now. Its most recent achievement was the capture of a 13½ lb salmon from the Itchen. The dressing is as follows:

Hook	No 10 long shank
Tails	A large bunch of pheasant-tail fibres, 12 or more, to keep the body floating horizontally
Body	A strip of polyethylene foam ribbed with the stalk of a natural red cock hackle
Hackle	Badger cock
Wings	Two bunches of slate-blue (dyed) cock hackle fibres, slanting forwards and divided as shown

This dressing seems to me to imitate the female imago before she is spent; it may be well to add another similar pattern, but with a light greenish-brown covering for the body (dyed PVC or raffene) and a greendrake (greenish-grey) coloured pair of wings. However, trout take the dressing given above even when eating sub-imagos.

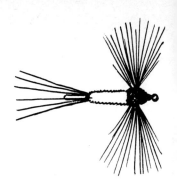

26 The Caenis Spinner

I do not pretend that this pattern is infallible when Caenis spinners are on the water—and, usually, on one's hat, jacket and spectacles, if worn. It will, however, catch some trout if cast accurately in front of individual fish, and it has the advantage of being very easy to tie.

I find it most effective when fished on a leader tapered to 2 lb bs, a No 5 fly-line and a rod chosen solely for accuracy; mine is an 8 ft split-cane. The fly must not be moved after it has alighted, until the fish at which it was aimed has either taken it or passed it; in the latter event, the fly is lifted off quickly and again put down a foot ahead of the cruising fish.

This is the dressing:

Hook	No 16
Tails and wings	White cock hackle fibres
Body	White swan herl
Thorax	Fine wool from a black lamb, which is actually sepia, dubbed on the silk
Tying silk	Dark brown

Tie in the wing fibres first, butts towards the hook bend. Cut off the butts slantwise, carry the silk down to the tail and tie in the tail fibres and two strands of swan herl. Wind the silk back, varnish it and, twisting the swan herl strands together, wind them over the still-wet varnish and tie in. Then divide the wing fibres into two well-spread horizontal bunches, with a figure-of-eight binding. Dub a little lamb's wool on the silk and wind to form the dark thorax. Finally, form the head and whip-finish.

27 Phase One

Some time ago, Mr A. J. D. Forest, of Lewisham, sent me samples of a fly he had devised and with which he has caught more than 100 trout in various fisheries. As you will see, it is another variation of the black hairwing theme, combining the substantial chenille body of Mr Bob Church's Black Chenille pattern with the touch of magenta found in the Sweeny Todd.

The dressing is as follows:

Hook   No 6 long shank
Wing, tail, throat hackle   Black squirrel hair
Body   Black chenille
Tying silk   Black

At the rear of the body, there are a few turns of neon-magenta DRF floss, followed by two turns of gold flat tinsel next to the tail.

The durability of the body is improved if you whip the hook-shank with the tying silk, then varnish this whipping and wind the body material while the varnish is still wet.

28 The Hatching Nymph

A recent article by Mr Geoffrey Bucknall reminded me of a pattern which I devised more than 20 years ago, and which I still use whenever trout are taking ephemerid nymphs on the point of hatching.

The principle can be applied to nymphs of any size or species and consists of tying-in a bunch of cock hackle fibres during the process of making the thorax. These fibres are set approximately vertical and the material that is to form the wing-cases is divided and brought forward so that each half lies on opposite sides of the bunch of hackle fibres.

The rest of the dressing is appropriate to the species of nymph to be imitated, while the bunch of hackle fibres is of a colour suitable to suggest the wing of the sub-imago.

The pattern is fished by doping the hackle fibres but not the rest of the fly, and avoiding drag in river fishing. On stillwaters, the smallest possible movement should be given. There are, however, occasions when the pattern is accepted by trout when completely sunk.

Mr Bucknall is quite correct in saying that there are times when the trout are taking only those insects that are in the act of ecloding, and then it is important to have patterns that suggest that state.

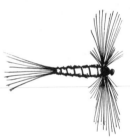

29 The Sherry Spinner

Here is a dressing for the Sherry Spinner that, though extremely successful, will not please professional fly-tyers! It involves materials which, though inexpensive and easily obtained, are not required for other patterns, and which therefore are not to be found in stocks.

The formula is as follows:

Tails and hackle Ginger cock. Use 10 or a dozen tail whisks, but only three or four turns of hackle

Wings Grey squirrel tail, or any hair of similar texture, dyed in blue dun (slate-grey) dye. Tie in a forward-facing bunch, and divide with figure-of-eight binding to set the fibres in two horizontal tufts

Body Very pale pheasant-tail fibres dyed hot-

orange, ribbed 3 lb bs clear nylon, also
dyed hot-orange

Tying silk	Hot orange
Hook	Size 14

30 Pepper's Own

Mr Anthony Pepper, of Pontefract, kindly sent me the pattern described hereunder, a dry fly that has been very successful on Yorkshire rivers. It rides well on streamy water, and obviously suggests the spinner stage of several common Ephemerid species.

Mr Pepper recommends size 14 for spring and 15 for later in the season. The larger size caught grayling in Hampshire in the last week of October.

The dressing is as follows:

Hook	14 or 15
Tails	Three strands of pheasant-tail fibre
Body	Three strands pheasant tail ribbed with bright red silk
Hackles	Natural red cock, with honey grizzle tied in front
Tying silk	Purple

The use of pheasant-tail fibres instead of the more usual cock hackle fibres for the tails does make the fly ride well, without the rear end tending to sink, and this idea may have application in other small dry-fly patterns.

31 Conservation Special

In this section I am deviating from my rule of describing only dressings that have accounted for at least 50 trout. The dressing is:

Body	Fur from the back of a Leadbetter's opossum, dubbed on white silk
Tail	About a dozen hairs from the back of a clouded leopard
Wing	A bunch of fibres from a takahé
Throat hackle	A breast feather from a New Zealand owl parrot
Cheeks	Jungle cock
Rib	Flat gold tinsel
Hook	No 4 long shank

This pattern is so far untried; but I am sure that anyone enterprising enough to secure the materials for it would be sure of success in almost any enterprise.

Some readers may care to exercise their minds in devising flies using even more difficult materials to obtain.

32 The Green Palmer

The first example of this fly that I ever saw was fixed firmly in the jaw of a trout weighing 5 lb, where it had been left on the previous day by Mr Guy Fletcher, who bet me £1 that I would not deliver the fish and fly to him. In that wager he showed me wisdom, for in the event of my failure he would win £1. Since I succeeded, he was able, in effect, to purchase a fresh-caught trout for 20p per lb, which must be a good buy anywhere.

I tied some flies to his pattern and found them very successful, especially when allowed to sink and then pulled steadily at a slow to medium speed.

The dressing is as follows:

Hook	Size 10 to 6
Body	Green seal fur dubbed on green silk
Hackle	A big cock hackle dyed light grass-green, wound palmer style
Rib	Fine gold thread. Wind this last so that it crosses the turns of hackle

The fly can be leaded or unleaded. In the first case, bind four or five layers of lead foil on the back of the hook-shank before putting on the rest of the dressing.

This pattern probably suggests a dragonfly larva.

33 The Short Orange Partridge

There is nothing new about the Orange Partridge. Indeed, it must be one of our oldest standard dressings, albeit a very useful one. I include it at the suggestion of the Editor of *Trout and Salmon,* since I caught an 18 lb trout on a special version of it.

Some years ago, when fishing Two Lakes as the guest of Lt-Col S. H. Crow, I became concerned with the problem of dealing with big trout that would accept only small flies. This problem was partly solved by tying a small fly 'short' on a comparatively large hook, on much the same principle as a low-water salmon fly. This style of dressing results in somewhat faster sinking without the added bulk of lead foil or piled copper wire.

Where outsize trout may be expected, the possible small

reduction in attractiveness is compensated by a much stronger hook-hold and the ability of the fly to go down to a cruising fish that you can actually see.

In case anyone does not know the dressing for the Orange Partridge, it is simply:

Body	Orange floss silk
Hackle	Brown partridge

But you can tie any pattern short, on a big hook.
Since the above pattern was devised a similar dressing has proved very successful when in hot weather green alga breaks away from lake bottoms and rises to the surface, carrying with it the green and brown larva of a species of midge.

The alternative pattern differs only from the original in having a body of phosphor yellow wool which in fact, despite its name appears lime green in colour. On one memorable occasion the author took four trout weighing 45 lb on this green bodied alternative.

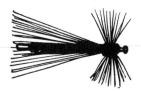

Plan view

34 The Hair Sedges

These patterns are the result of experiments I made in 1974 to develop flies that could be used by a gentleman who has the misfortune to be strongly allergic to feathers of any kind. The obvious alternative was hair, and a good many flies were developed, with the help of Miss Jacqueline Wakeford and Mr David Collyer. Among the most successful were some Sedges, which not only caught trout but were remarkably easy to tie.

The form of construction consists of first tying in a body in the usual way, then a bunch of hair, laid horizontally on the hook, in line with the shank, butts forwards. The butts are then divided and set horizontally at right angles to the hook-shank by means of a figure-of-eight binding. A refinement involves spinning a tiny amount of suitable fur on the silk for the last few turns of this figure-of-eight binding, after which the head is formed as usual. Finally, the three bunches of hair thus produced are clipped, the wing level with the hook-bend and the horizontal bunches quite short.

The two patterns so far found successful are:

Red Sedge

Hook	10
Body	Rabbit belly fur dyed chestnut with a very little orange DRF wool at the rear
Wing	Goat or similar hair dyed chestnut. Figure-of-eight dubbing, as body
Silk	Chestnut

Small Black Sedge

Hook	14
Body	Mole fur
Wing	Black squirrel hair. Dubbing as body
Silk	Black

We have found these patterns not only very attractive to trout, but also extremely durable and quick to dry after taking a fish.

Longhorns

35 Improved With Time

During the years since I began my series in *Trout and Salmon,* it is inevitable that some of the patterns described should have been improved upon, and I am indebted to many readers whose improvements have stood the test of practical fishing.

One development concerns Chompers and Long-horns—and, indeed, any other patterns using dyed ostrich

41

herl. This is very subject to fading, so it is better, if more time consuming, to replace it with a dubbing of fine dyed wool.

The body material for the Red Sedge can be chestnut pheasant-tail fibre instead of clipped dyed ostrich.

The only exception is the Sepia Dun Nymph, for which I have not yet found a satisfactory substitute for dyed ostrich. A pricked-out fur dubbing just doesn't look so natural in the water as ostrich herl.

All sorts of dressings have been given for Albert Whillock's very killing Whisky Fly. I do not find that it matters very much what the body, hackles or tails are made of, provided it has a good, bright orange wing, for which hair is much more durable than feather.

Nothing has proved anywhere near equal to the tandem Hanningfield Lure as a catcher of perch, including a lot of really big fish. This is the fly to use for perch on fly-only waters!

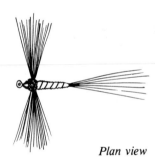

Plan view

36 Iron Blue Spinner

Many attempts have been made to imitate the female spinner of the iron blue, among the best-known being Lunn's Houghton Ruby, with hackle point wings, a wound hackle and a body of dyed cock hackle stalk. The dressing here recommended has a more translucent body.

Tails	Six to eight white hairs (fine goat hair or guard hairs from a white rabbit)
Body	One part magenta wool to two parts chestnut-dyed lamb's wool, thoroughly well mixed, ribbed crimson silk
Wings	Two bunches of slate-coloured fine hair

<table>
<tr><td>Thorax</td><td>(dyed) set horizontal and at right-angles to
hook-shank
Natural sepia lamb's wool</td></tr>
<tr><td>Silk</td><td>Crimson</td></tr>
</table>

The hairs for the wings are tied in, points forward, and left so while the waxed silk is taken to the start of the hook-bend, covering the butts of the wing hairs which are clipped slantwise. The tails are then tied in, together with the ribbing silk. The mixed body dubbing is applied to the silk, fairly thinly, and the body is wound and ribbed. The wing hairs are then divided by a figure-of-eight binding, to the last few turns of which is applied the sepia wool dubbing. This produces a dark thorax which should be a little fatter than the adjacent end of the body.

As a refinement, you can use crimson-dyed 2 lb bs nylon monofil instead of silk for the ribbing. There is no hackle.

37 Brown Damsel Nymph

Most imitations of damsel nymphs are greenish or olive, and these are often successful in stillwater trout fishing. However, many damsel nymphs are not green at all, but dark brown, and my observations lead me to think that this sort prefer to live near or among brownish weed, at the bottom.

An imitation that I have found very successful takes a little time to tie. The first operation consists in pinching a split shot on a No 10 or No 8 long shank hook, a little behind the eye. This is then painted brown with the kind of paint sold by car dealers for renovating tatty plastic covered upholstery. When the paint is dry, cover it with clear Vycoat, and let that dry as well.

Attach brown tying silk behind the shot, run it down to the commencement of the bend and there tie in four to six pheasant tail fibres and a length of 4 lb bs clear nylon monofil. Take the silk back to behind the shot, varnish the turns, and wind the pheasant fibres on to form a body, leaving their tips pointing backwards to form tails.

Rib the body with the monofil on an opposite spiral, and secure with a couple of half hitches, which you seal with varnish. Cut off the waste monofil but leave the butts of the pheasant fibres.

Attach the silk ahead of the shot, and tie in a throat hackle consisting of six to ten short pheasant fibres. Then bring the butts of the body fibres over the shot and tie down behind the eye, forming a head with the silk and ending with a whip finish.

Fish the pattern on a floating line and a long leader; let it sink, then try to work it back so that it bounces along the bottom.

38 The Fur Matuka

A reader in New Zealand, Mr Barry Dunkley, has kindly sent me samples of a type of fly that he tells me has been very successful there. I have no doubt that it will prove equally successful here, too.

The principle is similar to the well-known Matuka flies, except that instead of using a strip of feather on a split quill, a strip of suitable pelt is used, cut with scissors or a sharp blade.

The method of tying is to start the silk at the start of the hook-bend, tying in the body material, one end of the strip of pelt, and the ribbing. The silk is taken back to behind the eye, and the body material wound and secured. The strip of pelt is then brought forward, hair-side up, and secured with a few turns of silk at the head. The ribbing is then wound, separating the hair or fur into bunches—the strip of pelt must of course be hair-side upwards. There remains only to tie in the ribbing and finish the head in the usual way. I find it helps to damp the strip of pelt before tying it in, and to use very tight ribbing turns.

A wide range of patterns can be tied by this method, using floss, chenille, wool or dubbed bodies of various colours, a variety of different furs, and gold or silver ribbing.

One attractive version has a white DRF wool body, a flat silver tinsel rib and a strip of skin from the back of a brown hare. Don't use Lurex: it isn't strong enough.

39 The Roxton Flamingo

This is a fancy fly, the sort you carry in the fly-box to try when the trout won't take anything else. Such patterns often succeed in these circumstances, which occur mainly on heavily-fished waters where the trout have learned to avoid a large number of popular flies.

This is the dressing:

Hook	Down-eyed, 10 to 6
Body	White DRF floss or wool
Rib	Oval silver tinsel
Tail and hackle	Crimson cock hackle fibres
Wing	Feather-fibre from a soft pink flamingo feather, with a strip of teal over, or swan secondary feather-fibre dyed light salmon pink. Alternatively, a strip of bronze mallard can be used instead of teal

The throat hackle is tied in as a 'false hackle'. The fly should be lightly dressed.

As with all white or pale-bodied flies, it is advisable to varnish the hook-shank before starting the tie, to avoid iron-mould stain.

40 The Marabou Perch-Fry

I am indebted to Mr M. J. Clark, of Eastbourne, for this very successful pattern, which suggests a tiny perch. Mr

Clark caught large numbers of reservoir trout on it in 1975 and 1976, from mid-July onwards.

The dressing is as follows:

Hook	No 10 long shank, silvered
Body	Lightest silver grey chenille
Rib	Oval silver tinsel
Tail and throat hackle	Grey speckled mallard
Wing	Olive Marabou, rather sparse
Tying silk	White (keep it clean, or paint head white)

Tie in the throat hackle in two bunches, so as to spread well to each side.

When trout are attacking fry at the surface, try the Marabou on a floating line, with slow pulls and long pauses. If that fails, use a fast sinking line and fish the fly deep with a similar retrieve. Surface activity sometimes consists of killing the small fish, which are taken deeper down, after they have sunk.

41 Rabbit-Face Nymph

I am able to offer this pattern to British trout-fishers through the courtesy of its inventor, Mr Michael Jeavons, who hails from Hamilton, Ontario.

The dressing is as follows:

Hook	10 – 14
Tails	Brown partridge, short
Rib	Fine gold wire
Abdomen and thorax	Fur from between a wild rabbit's eyes, dubbed on olive silk
Wing cases	Feather-fibre from a dark speckled hen's feather, the kind used for Alders

Mr Jeavons finds a No 14 hook the most useful size. He prefers an unleaded version for river fishing, but says the same dressing over a leaded hook-shank can be useful for lakes.

42 Angora Grub

As well as being a very useful pattern for catching trout,
this is one that anybody can tie, even with no previous experience of fly-tying.

This is the formula:

Tying silk	Dark brown
Body	Angora knitting wool
Rib	Flattened clear nylon monofil, about 20 lb bs
Hook	No 8 long shank

I find the most successful colours for the Angora wool
are olive green, amber and almost any shade of brown.

Attach the silk behind the eye. Varnish the hook shank,
then run the silk to the beginning of the bend in open
spirals. At this stage, you may, if you wish, bind on any
number of strips from wine-bottle lead foil, from one to
seven, according to how heavy you want the fly to be.

If you have tied in lead, varnish over it. Then tie in the
wool and the flat monofil, and carry the silk back to the
eye. Wind on the wool, then the monofil rib on the
opposite spiral, secure and finish the head.

You can either wind the wool as it comes, or tease it out
and apply it as dubbing. In either case, prick it out on the
underside with a dubbing needle, between the turns of
ribbing.

Clip any loose hairs on the back as short as possible, then
give the back several successive coats of clear varnish. This
makes it very strong and resistant to trout teeth.

The grub will catch trout at any depth, but is particularly
effective when bumped slowly across the bottom on days
when no surface activity by the fish is apparent. This ap-
plies both in stillwaters and in rivers.

Monofil can be bought ready flattened, or you can flat-
ten it with a very hot iron, pressing it on a hard surface such
as Formica.

43 The Multistickle

The Multistickle consists of three Polystickles tied in tandem.

Take a No 6 long-shank round-bend hook and snip off the eye. At the bend of the hook using black silk, tie in a strip of PVC and a piece of Raffene, leaving the end of the Raffene to form a tail. To the shank of the hook whip a length of treble-plaited 6 lb bs nylon monofil, using white silk, first spiralling it along the shank, then binding down the plaited nylon with close turns. Varnish this binding. Then wind the black silk over it in open spirals. Near the head, tie in a piece of red wool. Wind this back one-third of the way towards the tail, then back over itself to the head.

Form the body by winding the PVC back and forth along the body to form a fish shape, stretching the PVC at the end of each layer of winding to avoid puckering. Finish at the head and tie in. Also tie in a throat hackle of orange cock hackle fibres.

Damp the Raffene, stretch it over the back and tie in. Form a head with the black silk and varnish. Put a touch of varnish at the tail-root.

Repeat with the second Polystickle and the third, this however being tied on a hook with the eye, preferably a straight one, retained. In the case of the third, front one, the surplus plaited nylon is cut off before finishing the dressing.

Theoretically there is no limit to the number of Polystickles you could use in this manner, but I suggest it would be difficult to cast with more than a dozen.

Colour Plates

In this section are included colour pictures relating to most of the patterns described in the volume. Some of the text sections do not lend themselves to illustration, which is the reason for the apparent gaps in the numbered captions. The flies were tied by Peter Gathercole, and photographed by Taff Price.

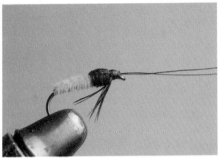

1 The Small Sedge Pupa

2 The Bumblebee

4 The Artificial Caddis

5   The Mayfly

7   The Yellow Corixa

8   The Mead Mill Special

9   The Leadhead

10   The Red-and-Black
     Midge Pupa

11   The Woolly B-W.O.

12   The Leaded DF Doll

13   The Jumbo Pupa

A New Mayfly Nymph

5   The Lamb's-Wool
     Damsel Nymph

16   Mother's Doormat

8   The Hairwing Spent Mayfly

20   Green Rabbits

51

21 Multi-Muddler

22 The Zero

23 The Blue Midge

24 The Ladybird

25 Russell's Mayfly

26 The Caenis Spinner

27 Phase One

28 The Hatching Nymph

The Sherry Spinner

30 Pepper's Own

The Green Palmer

33 The Short Orange Partridge

The Red Sedge

36 Iron Blue Spinner

Brown Damsel Nymph

38 The Fur Matuka

39 The Roxton Flamingo

40 The Marabou Perch-Fry

41 The Rabbit-Face Nymph

42 Angora Grub

44 The Undertaker

45 Nell Gwynne

48 Pond Olive Spinner

49 The Murk-Meister

54

44 The Undertaker

More people than ever before are taking up fly-tying, and for that reason I am always looking out for patterns that are not only effective, but easy to tie. I was, therefore, very grateful to Mr D. T. Dale, of Coventry, for this pattern.

The dressing is as follows:

Body Black wool, ribbed with very narrow silver tinsel

Back and tail Black wool

As will be seen from the illustration, the construction, apart from the ribbing, is the same as that for the well-known Baby Doll.

Mr Dale's sample is tied on a normal shank No 8 round-bend hook. I think it could be tied on a No 6 normal shank, or a No 6 or 8 long-shank. It sinks quite quickly, but if a faster-sinking rate is desired, some lead foil could be used under the wool. To improve its durability, the wool can be wound over wet varnish.

Mr Dale tells me the pattern has proved very effective over a wide range of retrieve rates, and has killed on all the Midlands lakes and reservoirs. Black and silver has always been an effective combination and I shall try the pattern with every confidence.

45 Nell Gwynne

I like to describe plenty of patterns that are easy to tie but effective for catching trout. This fly is a good example; anyone, even a complete beginner at fly-tying, can produce it.

The formula is as follows:

Hook	No 8 or No 6 long shank
Body	White DRF wool
Back and tail	Orange wool
Hackle	Orange dyed cock
Silk	Black

Tie in a rather long strand of white wool, a little behind the hook-eye. Varnish the shank to secure the dressing and to prevent iron-mould. Wind the wool in close turns to the start of the bend, where you use one turn of the wool to tie in the back material, which is a single strand of orange wool. Then wind the white wool back to where it was originally tied in; then back to the bend; then back again and tie down. In winding the white wool, adjust the closeness of turns to give a tapered effect.

Bring the orange wool forwards, nice and taut, and tie down behind the eye. Tie in an orange hackle, wind, secure and finish the head. Cut the tail to length and fluff it out. Apply varnish to the head and to the root of the tail to prevent the back material from slipping. For added fluorescent effect, rub the white wool turns with a bit of sand-paper, to fluff it up a bit.

The durability can be improved by soaking the back and

sides in clear varnish, but keep it off the hackle and the tail.

This pattern is a development of the Baby Doll. As Mistress Gwynne was a doll who became involved with oranges, the name may be thought appropriate!

The Cochan las

46 Claret and Sepia Duns

The naturals of these flies, *Leptophlebia marginata* and *Leptophlebia vespertina,* seem to be insects of waters that are on the acid side. The only water where I have observed them in the Midlands and southern England is at Two Lakes, in Hampshire, but they seem to be quite widespread in other districts, the claret dun being the commoner. Trout eat them keenly wherever they are found, unlike their near relation the turkey brown, *Paraleptophlebia submarginata,* which the fish do not care for at all.

The main difference between the sepia and claret duns is in size; the sepia is about as big as a spring olive *(Baetis rhodani)* while the claret is as large as an iron blue *(Baetis niger).*

Size can be deceptive where nymphs are concerned, the main distinguishing feature being the abdominal gills or ciliae. In the sepia nymph these are shaped like little Christmas trees, roughly triangular with their apexes outwards. In the claret nymph they are oval; shaped like water-lily leaves, but consisting of tiny radiating filaments. In both species these ciliae are much more pronounced than in the commoner nymphs of the pond olive *(Cloeon dipterum)* or the lake olive *(Cloeon simile)* and they have much longer tails, well spread out.

My original imitation of the sepia nymph, which proved very successful at Two Lakes, used sepia ostrich herl for the abdomen, ribbed with black floss, but I have modified this by using natural black sheep's wool, dubbed on black silk and ribbed with either black floss or black plastic strip; the latter looks more realistic, but I cannot find that the trout care which ribbing is used. The wool is pricked out in

57

generous tufts on each side of the abdomen, between the turns of ribbing, and then the tufts are levelled by clipping them back a little, until each tuft is the same length.

The tails, left very long, the wing cases, and the legs, are all of very dark pheasant-tail fibres. You can either dye a normal tail sepia, or look out for tails from melanistic cock pheasants, which are just right without dyeing. The thorax is black floss, fairly fat. You can dress this pattern as large as size 12 to imitate the sepia nymph, or on a 16 with the same materials for the claret nymph.

I would add in passing that the same pattern, but with lighter wool, darkish brown, tied on a No 8 or 10 long-shank, imitates the nymph of the summer Mayfly, *Siphlonurus armatus,* very well, but I never succeeded in catching trout on imitations of this insect at any stage.

C. F. Walker describes three species of summer Mayfly, *S. lacustris, S. linnearus* and *S. armatus.* I have observed the first on Loch Lomond and the last at Darwell, in Sussex, but I never saw a fish eat one of these insects. Walker gives dressings for nymph, dun and spinner, but I can only conclude that his dressings were never tried in actual fishing.

For a wet pattern to imitate the sepia and claret duns, Mr Mike Ashton refers me to a pattern he had from a colleague, Mr Maldwyn Evans, which has been very successful at Clywedog Reservoir and elsewhere. This is called the Cochan las, look you!, and the dressing consists of fairly long pheasant-tail whisks, a black dubbed wool body, well-tapered, a ginger Greenwell hen hackle and a very dark wing, which Mr Ashton thinks is cock blackbird secondary feather.

C. F. Walker recommends bronze mallard for the Sepia Dun wing and moorhen for the Claret Dun, when tied to fish dry, with a greyish-brown condor body and a sepia-dyed cock hackle. My own pattern for the dun uses the natural black sheep's wool—which is not really black—for the body, ribbed with black silk, and a bunch of very dark blue dun cock hackle fibres for the wing, with a gingery Greenwell hackle and sepia pheasant-tail fibres for the tails. This serves for both Sepia and Claret Duns; you simply slope the wing fibres back and use a hen Greenwell for the wet pattern, and slope the wing a little forward, with a Greenwell cock hackle, for the floating pattern. Wool is fine for dry-fly bodies now we have Permaflote to water-proof them; but you need the finest sheep's wool you can get, especially for the smaller, size 16, to imitate the Claret Dun.

For the spinners, it is preferable to use a lighter wool for the body, a warm brown mixed with black in equal parts being about right. Rib it with amber silk whose colour is fixed by soaking it in diluted Durofix, or use an amber-dyed cock hackle stalk. The wings can be two bunches of dark blue dun cock hackle fibres, set horizontal with the fibres well spread. With Permaflote you don't need a wound hackle, but you can add a couple of turns of short natural black cock if you like.

In the duns and spinners, a little added dubbing to thicken the thorax improves the silhouette, especially in the spinners, where you can prick it out a bit to imitate legs.

Mrs Palmer—note wing-length

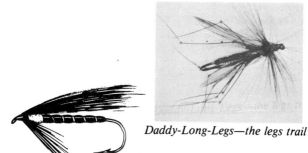

Daddy-Long-Legs—the legs trail

Sweeny Todd—crimson hackle

47 The Impostors . . .

Rudyard Kipling wrote: "If you can bear to hear the truth you've spoken, twisted by knaves to make a trap for fools. . ."

I am reminded of this when I see what happens to effective fly patterns that I, and others, have invented. They are described in books, and they crop up in tackle shops and tackle catalogues, bearing only a superficial resemblance to the originals.

About ten years ago, with helpful advice from Peter Thomas, I produced a fly called the Sweeny Todd. It is a most useful stillwater pattern, and if I had to be limited to a single pattern for reservoir trout fishing, I would choose it. The dressing is fairly simple; here it is:

Hook	Any size from 12 to two tandem size 6s; size 6 and 8 long-shank are perhaps the most useful sizes
Body	Black floss, ribbed fine silver thread (oval tinsel). Just behind the wing roots, take two or three turns of magenta DRF wool
Throat hackle	A false hackle of crimson-dyed cock hackle fibres
Wing	Black squirrel tail hairs
Tail	None

Now most of the books that describe the Sweeny Todd specify a magenta throat hackle instead of crimson. Many specify flat tinsel for the ribbing. And lately, the fly has started appearing in the tackle-shops with a red tail, which entirely defeats the object of putting magenta wool at the wing roots. So, in general, what is being described and sold as a Sweeny Todd, while it may catch fish, is certainly not the Sweeny Todd that Peter Thomas and I invented.

Tom Ivens' Jersey Herd is another example. The original pattern had an underbody of floss, built up to a fish shape and then covered with copper foil. I have never seen one in a shop that had a copper body. They all have gold bodies, and most of them do not have the underbody at all; just gold tinsel wound over a single layer of tying silk. Again, these things may catch fish, but they are not Jersey Herds.

My own Polystickle has suffered, too. It is rare indeed to find one in a shop in which the tying includes a spiral binding of black silk over a silvered hook-shank, or the alternative of silver tinsel in open spirals over a bronzed hook-shank, so that you get the appearance of a tiny translucent fish with its vertebrae showing through. And the tyers have now taken to making a tiny head no bigger than that of an ordinary fly, whereas one of the features of the original was a big, bold, built-up black head. As if that is not enough in the way of alteration, they have also decided to leave a tail twice as big as it ought to be, and to cut it forked. The original had a short tail, clipped square.

One of the minor breakthroughs of my fly-tying career was the discovery that an artificial Daddy-long-legs should have its legs trailing backwards, not spread out all round. In other words, imitate the fly as you see it either on the wing or drowned in the water, not as it is when it sits on your window-ledge.

An artificial tied with trailing legs is at least ten times more likely to catch trout than one with its legs spread out. I have explained this in numerous articles and in a little book called *Fly Dressing Innovations* which contains a full description of my Daddy-long-legs, together with two pictures of it, one a colour photograph and the other a black and white sketch.

Despite this, people continue to sell artificial Daddies with spread-out legs. Of course, other people have produced their versions of an artificial Daddy, and if they want to get it wrong, they're fully entitled to do so; but if they do, I'd be obliged if they would avoid selling it as my pattern—which they very frequently do. If it is going to be sold as Dick Walker's pattern, it should have eight backward-trailing pheasant-tail fibre legs, each knotted twice. And the wings should slant back, too, not be set out at right-angles to the body like a spent Mayfly.

As for Mayfly nymphs, I shall never cease to wonder at the extraordinary things that are tied and sold under that name. Their inventors and their tyers cannot possibly ever have seen a real Mayfly nymph, which is a large creature, a good inch long, whose predominant colour is a very pale yellowish buff, almost ivory, with dark brownish markings and wing-cases. Most of the alleged imitations I see look like scaled-up olive nymphs, and bear no resemblance to Mayfly nymphs at all.

I fish for grayling quite often in autumn and winter, mostly in Hampshire, and one of the most common flies on the chalk-streams in that county is the pale watery dun. Actually several species come under this heading, but one pattern of dry fly suffices for those that hatch in the part of the year when I am grayling-fishing.

I used to find the grayling difficult to catch during hatches of pale watery when I used the usual imitations, until I invented one of my own. It was tied with primrose silk of which three turns were exposed at the rear end of the body, and varnished to give a semi-translucent amber appearance. The body itself was very pale greenish-white. It

61

had so little green that you had to look carefully to see that any green was there at all.

Apart from flies tied by Miss Jackie Wakeford, I have never seen this pattern tied correctly. The exposed turns at the tail-end of the body are usually omitted, and the body is commonly bright green. As a matter of interest, I tried some of these wrong'uns on the grayling, which said, "We do not wish to know that; kindly leave the stage!" So here is a case where adulteration has made the pattern useless. Why? The fly was described in *Trout and Salmon;* it is in *Fly Dressing Innovations.* It is just as easy to tie it right as to tie it wrong. It costs no more, either.

Yet another pattern of mine that I have never seen tied correctly, except when I have tied it myself, is the hairwing Mrs Palmer. The original was tied thus:

Hook	Size 6 or 8 long-shank
Body	White DRF wool, ribbed fine silver thread, with a few turns of arc chrome DRF wool just behind the wing root
Throat hackle	A bunch of white cock hackle fibres
Wing	Very pale primrose fine goat hair, twice the length of the hook
Tail	None

This is a very useful pattern at times because it is attractive when retrieved very slowly, unlike many lure-type flies that need fast movement. It also does well in deeply-stained water.

I have never seen any but my own flies with wing hair of the right colour or length. It is usually bright yellow and no longer than the hook itself. And in a recently-published book, this fly has been given a tail, the body material changed to chenille, the ribbing changed to silver tinsel, the turns of arc chrome wool omitted, and the pattern described as having to be moved fast! I still remain credited with its invention, however!

It may be thought that my complaints are concerned largely with my own patterns. Not so: I have quoted these as examples because I know them so well. Other who devise flies suffer equally, if not more so. I can only suggest that anglers who wish to buy or tie the genuine article should beware of what is commonly on sale. Look up the original dressings and order from a professional fly-tyer if the local tackle-shop insists on offering unacceptable deviations.

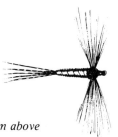

The Pond Olive Spinner viewed from above

48 Pond Olive Spinner

The Pond Olive *(Cloeon dipterum)* is the most common up-winged fly on most stillwater fisheries; though it may actually be exceeded in total number by one or other of the Caenis species, it is usually seen more often. Most anglers consider that to imitate the dun stage, a Greenwell is adequate, but no good imitation of the female spinner can be found in tackle-shops.

Spinners come back to the water late in the evening and I suspect many do so only after dark. When in the dusk rising trout refuse Sedges and Midge Pupae, a Pond Olive Spinner will often catch you a fish before the rules stop you fishing, and the following pattern is a good one:

Hook	14
Silk	Orange
Tails	Four or five strands of grey mallard feather fibre (speckled)
Body	Swan secondary fibre dyed the colour of tinned peaches, and wound over a varnished silk whipping while the whipping varnish is wet
Rib	Clear nylon monofil, 2 lb or 3 lb bs
Thorax	Chestnut pheasant tail
Wings	A bunch of dun hackle fibres divided by a figure-of-eight binding. The pheasant tail is wound over this binding
Hackle	None

Try to cast the fly in the path of rising fish, as nearly as can be judged. Do not pull it; let it lie inert until wind or drift cause it to drag. Then lift-off and cast again.

Trout taking spinners do so with little surface disturbance, but sometimes with a noise like a little kiss. It is quite unlike the slashing rise at sedges, or the surface cruising, with dorsal fin and tail-tip showing, that characterises the eating of midge pupae. If you suspect it, give the Pond Olive Spinner a try.

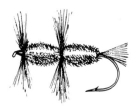

49 The Murk-Meister

This is a fly intended for use in stillwater trout fisheries whenever the water is thick with suspended matter, either mud stirred up by wave action or caused by excessive algal growth. The object is to ensure maximum visibility and at the same time produce a small disturbance that fish can detect.

The pattern has been well tried in the conditions for which it was devised and has proved very successful. It is in fact a development of a pattern devised by that prolific producer of effective patterns, Mr Richard Aylott. It should be retrieved in short, quick pulls with pauses between each pull.

The dressing is as follows:

Hook	Size 10, 8 or 6 long-shank
Tail	A tuft of white fluorescent wool
Bodies	Arc chrome (yellowish-orange) wool teased out and dubbed on the silk, built-up fat
Hackles	Stiff ginger cock hackles
Tying silk	Hot orange

The wool of the body should be well pricked-out with a dubbing needle when the fly is completed. It assists in bulking out the bodies if the white wool for the tail is tied in first, and then wound over the hook shank almost to the eye of the hook, the rest of the dressing being built up over this white wool base.

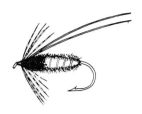

50 New-Style Longhorns

Some years ago, I devised what proved to be a most effective imitation of a sedge pupa coming up to hatch. In one or another of its four different colour combinations, this has caught a great many trout. However, it suffered from the disadvantage that the dyed ostrich herl used in its dressing soon faded through the combined effects of water and sunshine.

During the last three years, I have substituted dyed lamb's wool, dubbed on tying silk, for the ostrich herl. This has proved very successful, as the wool keeps its colour much better than the ostrich herl. It has to be dyed natural wool, however; knitting wool is not nearly as good.

The dressing is as follows:

Hook	Size 10 or 12, normal shank
Silk	Pale yellow
Body	Rear two-thirds amber *or* pale sea-green; front one-third sepia *or* chestnut, all of dyed natural sheep's wool. Rib, fine gold thread on rear half only
Hackle	Two turns short brown partridge
Horns	Two strands of pheasant-tail fibres slanting back over the hook cut to twice the length of the hook

This gives four colour combination, the choice of which depends on the species of sedge that is hatching. In order of which catch most fish for me, the colours are sepia and amber; sepia and green; chestnut and amber; chestnut and green.

When sedges are present in numbers but are not being taken on the surface, try a Longhorn. Don't be afraid to move it fairly fast, in a sink-and-draw action. It will kill even when the sedges are being taken on the surface, but it is more fun to use a dry fly then.

Some of my friends use bright crimson silk to finish the

head and claim this adds to the attraction of the pattern. I can only say that it certainly does not reduce it.

If you have to dye your own sheep's wool, of which you can find any amount in a field where there are sheep, you must degrease it first, in tepid water with plenty of detergent. A stock of this wool, dyed in a range of colours, is useful for a wide range of fly patterns.

Index